DOES THE BIBLE HAVE A VOTE IN MODERN DECISION MAKING?

"For the word of God is alive and active. Sharper than any double-edged sword, it penetrates even to dividing soul and spirit, joints and marrow; it judges the thoughts and attitudes of the heart."

—Heb 4:12 NIV

In today's strategic leadership environment, rarely is the spiritual dimension addressed as a resource to provide insights for leaders to make effective decisions that can be used to craft policy and strategy resulting in beneficial outcomes. What if there was a guidebook that leaders could use to help them make sound decisions that are also moral and ethical in today's ever-changing and uncertain environment? One possible guidebook of consideration is the Bible. When the United States was established as a country, the Founding Fathers created documents such as the Declaration of Independence, the Constitution and the Bill of Rights by utilizing a common thread or reference point, acceptance of a Judeo-Christian Ethic mindset originating from the Old and New Testaments within the Bible, to use as a standard to define policies of law, governance, social order and morality.[1] The point is not to prove or disprove whether the Founding Fathers were Christians but rather to acknowledge the evidence of their writings, statements, and actions that reflected Biblical principles as a foundation for a great nation.[2] Today, examples of Biblical references remain in American society: the many verses that adorn most of the Federal Buildings and Monuments in Washington D.C., phrases on the currency in circulation, the closing words in the Oaths of Office, the original Pledge of Allegiance, and the Ten Commandments engraved on the U.S. Supreme Court building— to name a few. This is not to infer by any means or to exclude other religious faiths that exist in America, but only offer a perspective from one of them.

While America has truly been blessed in its prosperity and world positioning, it appears that efforts of leadership to sustain these Judeo-Christian Ethic principles has steadily been declining since the Post WWII era and has gravitated towards a more secular and humanistic approach in defining moral and social standards to apply towards policy and strategy. Does this infer that the U.S. can expect changes to future outcomes that may be less than desirable or negative in nature? This paper will examine the strategic decisions, actions and policies of some notable current U.S. historical events to determine if Biblical principles have any correlation to their decision making process and outcomes.

The Bible as a Resource

Why should the Bible be considered as a possible resource for strategic decision making guidance? The first reason is because of credibility and availability. "The Christian Bible continues to be a revered book in the United States. In fact, no other book comes close to having been read and re-read as much as the "Good Book". Every year, millions of Bibles are printed in this country. Researcher George Gallup points out that so many Bibles have been printed in the United States that even rough estimates of the total number published to date do not exist."[3] A year 2000 Gallup Poll survey data indicated that 93 percent of Americans own at least one Bible.[4] While Bibles are commonly found in churches and book stores, they are often also seen in hotels, hospitals, schools, dentist's offices, colleges and universities, jails and prisons, military bases, and emergency worker stations.[5] The second reason is that the Bible provides a historical account and perspective of man's successes, failures and future prospects. The Biblical references used in this research paper are primarily focused on God's Ten Commandments because it provides a reference point, or in essence a benchmark, to compare and explain the outcomes of the historical examples to be presented based upon a construct of law and principles; while other Bible verses provide corollary supporting insights, principles, and possible consequences of actions.

U.S. Civil Rights

"Civil Rights" is a phrase of Latin origin called *ius civis* or the rights of citizens.[6] The issue of civil rights has been controversial in both policy and application. For example, in the United States following the end of World War II, key leadership decisions and legislative actions were made in attempts to end racial discrimination and segregation. On July 26, 1948, President Harry Truman signed Executive Order 9981 which ordered the integration of the armed forces, a bold move that bypassed the predominately white opposition representatives in Congress.[7] The 1954 U.S. Supreme Court case of Brown vs. the Board of Education of Topeka, Kansas was a milestone judicial decision by the Court declaring state laws were unconstitutional in establishing separate public schools for black and white students.[8] The Civil Rights Act of 1964 started as a proposed bill initiated by President Kennedy during his civil rights speech on July 11, 1963.[9] The efforts of prominent civil rights leader Martin Luther King Jr. and the March on Washington on August 28, 1963 helped provide the catalyst for the bill as it passed legislation the following year. It became the pivotal benchmark that led social change in the U.S. as a lawful means to end discrimination against blacks and women, including racial segregation in schools, the workplace, and other public venues.

Why did these leaders pursue many efforts to establish these civil rights policies and why were they successful? One possible explanation may be their personal courage and motivation of duty as leaders to do what's right such as it is reflected by the Founding Fathers writings in the Declaration of Independence stating that "We hold these truths to be self-evident, that all men are created equal, that they are endowed by their Creator with certain unalienable Rights, that among these are Life, Liberty and the pursuit of Happiness."[10] The statement that all men are created equal proposes that men are brothers living together in harmony with mutual respect for each other. In the Bible, the verse "Love your neighbor as yourself" Mt 22:39 NIV is what type of relationship God wants people to have among people. For the strategic leader, this Biblical principle can provide an inner perspective of how he or she defines the world and their purpose of relationship among people they lead, follow and collaborate with.

Roe vs. Wade

The famous and controversial judicial decision of the 1973 U.S Supreme Court to legalize abortion in the case of Roe vs. Wade continues today to divide the U.S. population over moral and ethical situational dilemmas. The Court upheld that a woman has a right to an abortion up until viability of the unborn fetus. The Roe decision defined "viable" as being "potentially able to live outside the mother's womb.[11] Other than circumstances that were life-threatening to the baby or mother, this decision allowed a woman the latitude to abort a pregnancy based upon her values of convenience over the life or potential life she carries.

Since the Roe vs. Wade decision in 1973 and up to 2008, 53,310,822 abortions have been documented in the U.S at a current average rate of 1.2 million abortions a year.[12] Studies indicate that women who have undergone an abortion procedure can experience a five to ten year period of psychological trauma as well as physiological trauma that can affect future fertility.[13] This data translates that the U.S. as a nation within the life span of half a generation, being about 35 to 40 years, killed these

4

potential people that would have been a viable replacement workforce to provide for the future growth and productivity, especially when the preceding "Baby Boom" generation is about to retire. If abortion had not been legalized in 1973, the 2008 Social Security contribution amount provided by this lost population would have been over $47 billion dollars, more than enough to cover the 2011 Congressional Budget Office Social Security deficit estimate of $45 billion dollars.[14] The hard reality is that Roe versus Wade was a strategic decision made by leaders in the Judicial Branch of the government to legalize a mindset and practice that allowed its people to perform abortions, or murders of convenience. "According to former Surgeon General, Dr. C. Everett Koop, the most common reason for abortion is convenience. Only three to five percent of all abortions performed are for reasons of rape, incest, the possibility of a deformed child, or severe threat to the life of the mother. In other countries, such as China and India, where male babies are favored over female babies, the abortion and infanticide of girls has led to a severe shortage of brides for young men."[15] It appears that abortion destroys the human resources that are vital to a country's future needs.

The Roe vs. Wade abortion issue can be framed in the Sixth Commandment, "You shall not murder" Ex 20:13 NIV. In this Biblical context, God is the creator and sustainer of human life, therefore man should value and protect the lives of all innocent humans.[16] From the moment of conception, God is involved and cherishes every life, "For You created my inmost being; You knit me together in my mother's womb" Ps 139:13 NIV. "Pre-natal human life is fully human and thus precious to God."[17] Strategic leaders that disregard the sanctity of human life may incur similar follow-on implications and consequences that could seriously impact the socio-economic future of generations to come.

The Watergate Scandal

In the case of President Richard Nixon and the Watergate Scandal of 1972, the lie he committed had significant national consequences that shook the foundation of the U.S. Government for years to follow. The scandal began when "burglars" broke into the Democratic National Committee headquarters located within the Watergate building complex on June 17, 1972 in an attempt to steal privileged information to discredit Daniel Ellsberg, a RAND Corporation analyst who leaked to the press a classified Pentagon study that revealed secret U.S. policy decisions made during the Vietnam War.[18] The "burglars" were arrested and the FBI linked them to a financial source used by a Committee to Re-elect the President.[19] An investigation was conducted by the Senate Watergate Committee where it gathered evidence and testimonies against President for secretly recording conversations from within his office that would implicate him as having knowledge of a break-in.[20] During the proceedings; President Nixon denied any knowledge or involvement of any government individuals or agencies. It was not until a critical tape recording was discovered and released that proved otherwise.[21] Instead of confronting impending impeachment procedures, Nixon resigned as President on August 9, 1974. Following Nixon's resignation, Gerald Ford succeeded as President and pardoned Nixon.

The consequences of President Nixon's personal decision to lie not only cost him his presidency, the aftermath of the Watergate Scandal propagated the American public's mistrust in their government. In addition to Nixon, other senior officials involved were lawyers, the scandal created a negative public image perception of the legal profession.[22] The President having being accused of involvement in criminal activity led the public to question the moral integrity of its senior leaders. Even today, people remain skeptical and negative whether politicians are serving themselves or the people that elected them.

"You shall not bear false testimony against your neighbor" Ex 20:16 or the act of lying is the Ninth Commandment and probably the most commonly broken law by all people. Whether the lie is small or large, there are consequences that leaders must be held personally accountable for. Nixon's deception resulted in him being chastised, mentally depressed, and having a political career ending in disgrace. It appears that the Bible has a corollary description of the outcomes, "The LORD will send on you curses, confusion and rebuke in everything you put your hand to, until you are destroyed and come to sudden ruin because of the evil you have done in forsaking Him" Dt 28:20 NIV. Strategic leaders can learn from this example as self-examination to determine if their own integrity is one of truth above reproach.

The End of the Cold War

The Cold War was a protracted political and economic duel between two superpowers, the United States and the Soviet Union each jockeying for worldwide influence spanning over forty years. The culmination of this confrontation came to a close near the end of President Reagan's second term in office.[23] Although history often credits Reagan as the instrumental figure that ended the conflict; critics still debate the merits or methods he used to bring resolution. While many believe that Reagan's expansive defense policies, hard line rhetoric tactics against the Soviet Union and Communism, and personal negotiations with General Secretary Gorbachev were the means used in ending the Cold War, others believe the collapse of the Soviet Union was inevitable no matter who was in power.[24]

The overall success of President Regan's efforts can be summed up by Margaret Thatcher, former Prime Minister of the United Kingdom, who said "Ronald Reagan had a higher claim than any other leader to have won the Cold War for liberty and he did it without a shot being fired."[25]

In a speech President Reagan made to the Student Congress on Evangelism at the Washington Convention Center on July 28, 1988, about a year prior to the fall of the Berlin Wall, he revealed his position on the Soviet Union and the Communist world from his religious perspective of hope and prayer stating, "Today there are profound changes underway in the Communist world. My trip to Moscow convinced me of that. And of all the changes underway, perhaps none holds more hope for the future than Mr. Gorbachev's statements that the Soviet Union would soon grant its believers certain new freedoms. But while we pray for those inside the Communist world, we must cherish the freedoms that we already enjoy, cherish a nation founded in freedom. Just think of those words we recited a few moments ago. The Pledge of Allegiance asserts that our nation is under God—an unthinkable statement in too many countries around the world today. And it proclaims the ideals of liberty and justice, ideals that we may not have completely achieved but that as a free people we're constantly striving toward."[26]

"British historian M. J. Heale, who finds that scholars now concur that Reagan rehabilitated conservatism, turned the nation to the right, practiced a pragmatic conservatism that balanced ideology and the constraints of politics, revived faith in the presidency and in American self respect, and contributed to victory in the Cold War."[27]

The First Commandment "I am the Lord your God." Ex 20:2 NIV is reflection indicative of Reagan's acknowledgement and belief in God. "Reagan publically stated that he was a born-again Christian. In private and public statements, his expressed views on doctrinal matters agree with the teachings of orthodox Christianity. Perhaps more than any other president in recent history, Reagan's religion influenced his presidency - and the nation - in a positive way."[28] President Reagan is an example of a strategic leader that believed in God and used the Bible as a means to guide his decision making process on policies and strategies. Was he always successful? No, but those endeavors that were apparently aligned with God's plan were blessed.

The Lewinsky Scandal

In January 1998, President Bill Clinton admitted that he had an "improper relationship" but lied that he had sexual relations with a White House intern named Monica Lewinsky.[29] The scandalous affair and its repercussions led to impeachment hearings. The Senate conducted a three week trial that resulted in insufficient votes for a Constitutional two-thirds majority requirement to convict and remove the President from office based upon the charges of perjury and the obstruction of justice.[30] The event brought to issue the discussion among the American public whether the moral character of a public figure has any relevance of their capacity to do the job they were elected to perform. This mindset would further promote that no absolute moral values exist or apply to public officials notwithstanding the average citizen. The impact of the President's action exemplified the fact that a leader can have an adulterous affair and still remain in office while being morally unaccountable to the public he serves. But because he repented publically to the nation for his adulterous behavior,[31] he may have been spared from prolonged scrutiny by the American public. Although Bill Clinton was not the first U.S. President to have an extramarital affair while in office, his personal behavior and notoriety became a more publically acceptable norm that what a political leader does in private has no correlation to their performance of what they do as an elected official.

The Seventh Commandment, "You shall not commit adultery" Ex 20:14 NIV is God's law established to preserve the sanctity of the marriage relationship between one man and one woman from being undermined by sexual impropriety. The outcomes of adultery can lead to acts of lying, stealing, physical and emotional abuse and even murder as documented in the Bible's recording of the relationship between King David and Bathsheba. Eventually, sexual impropriety results in hurting not only those involved but also family and friends. As a leader it could impact credibility and trust among followers and organizations. For those who believe in God and His word, "Marriage should be honored by all, and the marriage bed kept pure, for God will judge the adulterer and all the sexually immoral." Heb 13:4 NIV

The ENRON Scandal

"The ENRON Corporation was formed in 1985 by its founder and chairman Kenneth Lay after merging the two utility companies of Houston Natural Gas and InterNorth. Several years later, he and ENRON's president and CEO Jeffrey Skilling developed a staff of executives that, through the use of accounting loopholes, special purpose entities, and poor financial reporting, were able to hide billions in debt from failed deals and projects."[32] "Enron's shareholders lost $74 billion in the four years before the company's bankruptcy ($40 to $45 billion was attributed to fraud)."[33] Lay, Skilling and other executives were convicted of fraud. Lay died before his sentencing.

The ENRON scandal is an example of corporate fraud committed by senior leaders on a grand scale that affected shareholders, employees and the public trust and accountability of big business companies. The Eighth Commandment, "You shall not steal" Ex 20:15 NIV means to "prohibit all acts of misappropriation."[34] The teaching point here is that leaders must be good stewards of the resources entrusted to them in order to provide for the welfare of their people. If they lose sight of this purpose, their motives and intent may lead them down the path of stealing and corruption. Here are two possible Biblical outcomes for stealing, the first being a corrective measure; "Anyone who has been stealing must steal no longer, but must work, doing something useful with their own hands, that they may have something to share with those in need" Eph 4:28 NIV. The second possible outcome is the punishment of failure, financial ruin, imprisonment and destruction which were incurred by those convicted in the ENRON scandal. The Bible has parallel descriptions for these outcomes, "The LORD will send on you curses, confusion and rebuke in everything you put your hand to, until you are destroyed and come to sudden ruin because of the evil you have done in forsaking Him." Dt 28:20 NIV, "At midday you will grope about like a blind person in the dark. You will be unsuccessful in everything you do; day after day you will be oppressed and robbed, with no one to rescue you." Dt 28:29 NIV and "He will put an iron yoke [imprisonment] on your neck until he has destroyed you." Dt 28:48b NIV

The U.S. Financial Crises of 2007

The U.S. Financial Crisis of 2007 is an event that affected the nation on such a grand scale that many economists called it "the worst financial crisis since the Great Depression of the 1930s."[35] The crisis began from a shortage of liquid assets among U.S banks which required a federal government bailout of collapsing financial institutions that in turn created a downturn in the world stock markets.[36] These conditions caused a chain reaction that cost the U.S. trillions of dollars in reduced consumer spending wealth, crippled the housing market, contributed to failed business ventures, increased unemployment, induced a slowed economy and significantly increased foreign debt.[37] But who was responsible for the crisis? In this case, it was a collective action of leaders and citizens who at all levels overextended themselves beyond their fiscal means.

Ever since people as children became jealous of their sibling's or neighbor's possessions, man has developed a tendency to focus on his wants rather than on his needs. The Tenth Commandment "You shall not covet" means that a person should not be envious or greedy of his fellow man's possessions or status and have underlying motives to attain these from him.[38] Modern advertising floods consumers daily with what they perceive people need more of to make them happy, powerful and successful…otherwise known as excess or greed. The Bible states that God blesses each person to live within the means that He deems them capable of. "Keep your lives free from the love of money and be content with what you have, because God has said, "Never will I leave you; never will I forsake you." Heb 13:5 NIV Losing sight of these principles may result in these consequences, which are similar to those depicted in the Bible, "Your basket [purchasing power] and your kneading trough [productivity] will be cursed" Dt 28:17 NIV, "You will build a house, but you will not live in it." Dt 28:30b and "You will plant a vineyard [business], but you will not even begin to enjoy its fruit [profit]." Dt 28:30c NIV Leaders can glean wisdom from this by being fiscally responsible in their decisions and actions that provide benefits commensurate with the needs of people they serve.

The McChrystal Resignation

General Stanley McChrystal was the Commander of the International Security Assistance Force (ISAF) and Commander, U.S. Forces Afghanistan (USFOR-A) from June 15, 2009 to June 23, 2010. It is of opinion that General McChrystal was selected by the President Obama for the challenging assignment because of his reputation of speaking boldly for needed resources to resolve the Afghanistan situation where others were afraid to speak up.[39] McChrystal became the center of controversy when an article in Rolling Stone magazine titled "the Runaway General" was released to the public. The article portrayed McChrystal and his staff as making derogatory remarks against civilian government officials, to include the Vice-President Joe Biden.[40] While McChrystal was not personally quoted as being critical of the president and his policies, the comments offered by his aides provided a perception that he was not in agreement with the administration's direction of Afghan policy decisions.[41] McChrystal apologized to Vice-President Biden[42] and issued a statement taking personal responsibility for his mistake in judgment.[43] General McChrystal was summoned back to Washington, D.C. where he met with President Obama and handed the President his resignation.[44] Shortly thereafter General McChrystal announced his retirement.[45]

The Fifth Commandment "Honor Your Father and Your Mother" Ex 20:12 NIV extends its meaning of respect and honor to those in authority. God ordains authority to those leaders that are responsible for the people they serve. In General McChrystal's case, he was subject to the authority of his Commander-in-Chief, President Obama. While McChrystal may have allowed his staff to disrespect the president and the

13

leaders, he was honorable to accept the personal responsibility for the incident by demonstrating respect by means of his resignation. While unfortunate that such a well-qualified leader was removed from leadership duties, strategic leaders must be able to voice constructive and truthful opinions in confidence while providing the respect and honor that their superiors are entitled.

The Rest and Recuperation Leave Program

The Rest and Recuperation Leave Program was established in 2003 and first utilized in the U.S. Central Command Area of Operations to provide the opportunity for U.S. service members and Department of Defense civilians who were deployed in the combat theater for 1 year to take up to 15 days of leave during their deployment.[46] The program provided an interval relief cycle of rest and recreation period for the service member from the stresses associated with combat and allowed them to reunite with family and friends when they returned home. The military saw it as an important investment in preserving the well-being of the forces and a way to improve overall mission performance.[47]

The Fourth Commandment "Remember the Sabbath day by keeping it holy" Ex 20:8 NIV gives a prescribed day of rest as a pattern of life that conforms to the nature of God.[48] In Biblical context, God rested on the seventh day after He created the heavens and earth. Rest is a required function to rejuvenate the body, mind and soul. Serving in the military especially in a combat environment can be extremely stressful and it is a leader's responsibility is to ensure his troops and himself to get the required rest to be effective and mission capable. The military's strategic decision to implement this Rest and Recuperation Leave program was a successful effort in taking care of the troops that reflected God's principle.

<u>"Cyber-Bullying"</u>

"Cyber-bullying has been defined as "when the Internet, cell phones or other devices are used to send or post text or images intended to hurt or embarrass another person" [49] In 2006, Megan Meier, an American teenager committed suicide as a result of cyber-bullying that was conducted via a social network website called MySpace.[50] This incident drew national attention and initiated legislation in seven states to make cyber- bullying illegal. On March 10, 2011 at a White House conference on bullying prevention, President Obama addressed an audience of students, parents, teachers, and civic leaders stating that bullying in schools and online is a national problem. [51] "A third of middle school and high school students have reported being bullied during the school year," Obama said. "Almost 3 million students have said they were pushed, shoved, tripped, even spit on. It's also more likely to affect kids that are seen as different, whether it's because of the color of their skin, the clothes they wear, the disability they may have, or sexual orientation."[52] According to a Department of Education source, such students who participate in bullying are prone to have more school challenges, drug and alcohol abuse, to include health and mental problems.[53] He warned how new social media network technologies such as FaceBook and MySpace can be misused by cyber-bullies to reach their victims. "Bullying can have destructive consequences for our young people. And it's not something we have to accept."[54] President Obama directed the creation of a new federal website aimed to address the issue.[55]

The Third Commandment "You shall not misuse the name of the Lord your God" Ex 20:7 refers to the profanity of speech and any attempt to manipulate God's name to further human plans.[56] In Biblical context, God gave man the ability to speak and write, therefore taking the Lord's name in vain or swearing dishonors Him and the people He created. Profanity can be prevented only if people make a conscious effort to do so. Cyber-bullying is a modern means of profanity with the sole intent of hurting people. There are no benefits that can result from this negative behavior. Propriety in what a leader says and how he says it can establish a positive example and tone for his subordinates to follow just as President Obama did for the nation.

The Army Seven Core Values

When the U.S. Army Training and Doctrine Command (TRADOC) published the Army Seven Core Values back in 1998, it not only defined the standards for conduct and behavior for the Army but also for the society that it draws its future recruits from.[57] These seven core values of loyalty, duty, respect, selfless-service, honor, integrity and personal courage have been part of an indoctrination process for all soldiers, non-commissioned officers, and officers to uphold as the defining character traits that binds the Army together as a team.[58] The origins of these values are tied to the American culture and beliefs that centers on freedom, respect of individual expression, sacrifice for others and the support of lawful governance towards the nation. The moral and ethical good are reflected in the essence of America's character through the legacy of its forefathers. After almost ten years of continuous operations in both Iraq and Afghanistan, the Army values became the cornerstone that allowed the Army to sustain and endure the rigors of combat, transformation and the current challenges of significant budget and equipment reductions.

The Second Commandment "You shall have no other gods before me" Ex 20:3 NIV refers to idol worship of something or somebody that takes the place of God.[59] In ancient days people made idols of stone, wood or metal that represented their values.

They would sacrifice their time, money, resources, and even family to worship these god idols in attempts to gain favor or success. In Biblical context, God condemns this practice for He requires man to value Him the creator not the products of creation. In America today, the idols of the past are now replaced with present substitutes such as the love of money and possessions, the fanaticism of sports and entertainment celebrities, the addiction to alcohol, drugs, gambling, and pornography, the excessive dependence of technology and connectivity of the internet, and tyranny of busyness— filling the calendar with events and activities without stop—all for self-centric reasons to provide meaning and purpose in life. The Army Seven Core Values has proven to be a successful strategic decision for its organization of people to uphold the basic fundamental principles focused on servant leadership that are aligned with the original moral and ethical values reflected throughout the Bible. This mantle of responsibility rests on the shoulders of America's future leaders.

Conclusion

Upon initial examination of the historical examples presented, strategic decisions and actions can result in positive or negative outcomes based upon the character and motives of the leaders making them. What was the guiding source of reason they utilized in their decision-making process? Some may cite that it was their innate skills, experience, personal fortitude or fate that determined the results of their situations. Whether it was an individual or collective effort, each case had alternative options or paths that were available for consideration. As with any decision there are inherent risks and consequences that usually remain unseen and unpredictable. Nobody deliberately plans to fail, especially when the stakes are high, but some do fail possibly due to improper intent and expectations. Because man is human and therefore fallible, he often compensates by self-defining standards of right and wrong based upon his position or perspective in life. In the historical examples where there was apparent success, those leaders, policies or decisions may have aligned with the values and virtues that were of selfless service and piety. The other historical examples that ended in failure may have been based on egos and self-serving agendas.

Does the Bible have a vote in modern decision-making? The relevance of utilizing the Bible and the Ten Commandments, to correlate its enduring principles and outcomes, does suggest possible conclusions can be drawn to provide a strategic leader an optimal means to frame and make decisions that have a grounded moral and ethical reference base. Given the world's ever-changing and uncertain situations, it may be a prudent endeavor to further explore the many other facets of the Bible's contents which may provide additional insights of wisdom for the future.

Endnotes

[1] Richard G. Lee, Dr., The American Patriot's Bible, The Word of God and the Shaping of America (Nashville: Thomas Nelson, Inc, 2009), Preface, "The Seven Principles of the Judeo-Christian Ethic"

[2] Ibid.

[3] George Gallup, Jr., The Role of the Bible in American Society (Princeton: The Princeton Religion Research Center, 1990) http://www.theologicalstudies.org/page/page/1572910.htm (accessed March 1, 2011).

[4] In 2000, Gallup conducted a survey for the American Bible Society (ABS), with the intent to discover trends in Bible readership. http://www.gallup.com/poll/6217/Word-BibleBuying.aspx (accessed March 1, 2011).

[5] Gideons International, Minstrywatch.com, http://www.ministrywatch.com/profile/Gideons-International.aspx (accessed March 1, 2011).

[6] Civil and political rights, Wikipedia, http://en.wikipedia.org/wiki/Civil_and_political_rights (accessed February 4, 2011).

[7] Executive Order 9981, Wikipedia, http://en.wikipedia.org/wiki/Executive_Order_9981 (accessed February 4, 2011).

[8] Brown v. Board of Education, Wikipedia, http://en.wikipedia.org/wiki/Brown_v._Board_of_Education (accessed February 4, 2011).

[9] Radio and Television Report to the American People on Civil Rights, June 11, 1963. http://www.jfklibrary.org/Research/Ready-Reference/JFK-Speeches/Radio-and-Television-Report-to-the-American-People-on-Civil-Rights-June-11-1963.aspx (accessed February 5, 2011).

[10] The Declaration of Independence, U.S. History.org, http://www.ushistory.org/DECLARATION/document/index.htm (accessed February 6, 2011).

[11] Mary Wood, and Lisa Hawkins, "State Regulation of Late Abortion and the Physician's Duty of Care to the Viable Fetus", 45 Mo. L. Rev. 394 (1980)

[12] Based on numbers reported by the Guttmacher Institute 1973-2008, with estimates of 1,212,400 for 2009-2010. GI estimates a possible 3% under reporting rate, which is factored into the total. http://www.nrlc.org/abortion/facts/abortionstats.html (accessed January 3, 2011).

[13] David C. Reardon, PhD., "The Aftereffects of Abortion", Elliot Institute, http://www.abortionfacts.com/reardon/after_effects_of_abortion.asp (accessed January 3, 2011).

[14] "Economic Impact of Abortion", http://www.nrlc.org/factsheets/FS04_MissingPersons.pdf (accessed January 3, 2011).

[15] Michael Monahan, Heritage House '76, *Abortionfacts* "Special Message", January 24, 2004, http://www.abortionfacts.com/bible/pastor_cole.asp (accessed January 3, 2011).

[16] Ibid.

[17] Ibid.

[18] Egil Krogh, (June 30, 2007). "The Break-In That History Forgot". *New York Times*. http://www.nytimes.com/2007/06/30/opinion/30krogh.html (accessed January 3, 2011).

[19] Watergate.info, June 23, 1972., http://www.watergate.info/tapes/72-06-23_smoking-gun.shtml (accessed January 3, 2011).

[20] Narrative by R.W. Apple, Jr.; chronology by Linda Amster; general ed.: Gerald Gold. (1973). *The Watergate Hearings: Break-in and cover-up; proceedings*. New York: Viking Press. http://www.worldcat.org/oclc/865966&referer=brief_results. (accessed January 3, 2011).

[21] "Watergate Scandal", Wikipedia, http://en.wikipedia.org/wiki/Watergate_scandal (accessed January 3, 2011)

[22] Ibid.

[23] "Reagan's legacy". *The San Diego Union Tribune*. June 6, 2004. http://www.signonsandiego.com/uniontrib/20040606/news_lz1x6legacy.html. (accessed March 1, 2011).

[24] Roger Chapman (June 14, 2004). "Reagan's Role in Ending the Cold War Is Being Exaggerated". George Mason University. http://hnn.us/articles/5569.html. (accessed Mar 1, 2011).

[25] "Reagan and Thatcher; political soul mates". MSNBC. June 5, 2004. http://www.msnbc.msn.com/id/5145739/ (accessed March 2, 2011).

[26] President Reagan's address to the 1988 Student Congress on Evangelism at the Washington Convention Center on July 28, 1988, http://ronaldreagansfaith.com/5.html. (accessed March 5, 2011).

[27] M.J. Heale, Cheryl Hudson, and Gareth Davies, eds. *Ronald Reagan and the 1980s: Perceptions, Policies, Legacies* (2008) Palgrave Macmillan, 250.

[28] Daniel J. Mount, *The Faith of America's Presidents* (Chattanooga: Living Ink Books/AMG Publishers, 2007), 35.

[29] Peter Baker; John F. Harris (August 18, 1998). "Clinton Admits to Lewinsky Relationship, Challenges Starr to End Personal 'Prying'". *The Washington Post*: p. A01. http://www.washingtonpost.com/wp-rv/politics/special/clinton/stories/clinton081898.htm. (accessed January 3, 2011).

[30] "How the senators voted on impeachment". CNN. February 12, 1999. http://edition.cnn.com/ALLPOLITICS/stories/1999/02/12/senate.vote/. (accessed January 3, 2011).

[31] President Clinton's Address to the Nation, August 17, 1998, at PBS.org, http://www.pbs.org/newshour/lewinsky_address/address.html, (accessed January 3, 2011).

[32] ENRON Scandal, Wikipedia, http://en.wikipedia.org/wiki/Enron_scandal, (accessed December 29, 2010).

[33] Ibid.

[34] John Bowker, *The Complete Bible Handbook* (New York: DK Publishing, 2001), 57.

[35] Three top economists agree 2009 worst financial crisis since great depression; risks increase if right steps are not taken. (February 29, 2009). http://www.reuters.com/article/2009/02/27/idUS193520+27-Feb-2009+BW20090227 (accessed December 1, 2010).

[36] Financial crisis (2007–present), Wikipedia, http://en.wikipedia.org/wiki/Financial_crisis_of_2007%E2%80%932010 (accessed December 1, 2010).

[37] "Brookings-Financial Crisis" (PDF). http://www.brookings.edu/~/media/Files/rc/papers/2009/0615_economic_crisis_baily_elliott/0615_economic_crisis_baily_elliott.pdf. (accessed December 1, 2010).

[38] Bowker, *The Complete Bible Handbook*, 57.

[39] Peter Beaumont, (2009-09-27),"Stanley McChrystal: The president's stealth fighter", London: The Guardian (UK). http://www.guardian.co.uk/theobserver/2009/sep/27/stanley-mcchrystal-commander-us-forces. (accessed March 15, 2011).

[40] Michael D. Shear, Ernesto Londoño and Debbi Wilgoren (June 22, 2010). "Obama to meet with McChrystal before making 'any final decisions' on dismissal". *The Washington Post*. http://www.washingtonpost.com/wp-dyn/content/article/2010/06/22/AR2010062200813_pf.html. (accessed March 15, 2011).

[41] Mark Urban, (June 22, 2010). "What's behind McChrystal Obama 'Rolling Stone' row?", BBC News, http://www.bbc.co.uk/blogs/newsnight/markurban/2010/06/general_stanley_mcchrystal_has.html (accessed March 15, 2011).

[42] David Gura, (June 23, 2010). "On Monday Night, McChrystal Called Biden To Apologize For Remarks In Profile". NPR. http://www.npr.org/blogs/thetwo-way/2010/06/23/128027916/on-monday-night-mcchrystal-apologized-to-biden-for-remarks-in-profile. (accessed March 15, 2011).

[43] Peter Spiegel, (June 21, 2010). "McChrystal on Defensive for Remarks". Wall Street Journal. http://blogs.wsj.com/washwire/2010/06/21/mcchrystals-next-offensive/. (accessed March 15, 2011).

[44] Shaun Waterman, (June 23, 2010). "Obama accepts McChrystal's resignation". Washington Times, http://www.washingtontimes.com/news/2010/jun/23/mcchrystal-leaves-white-house-war-meeting/ (accessed March 15, 2011).

[45] Annie Gearan (June 28, 2010). "Stanley McChrystal Retiring From The Army After Firing By Obama". *The Huffington Post*. http://www.huffingtonpost.com/2010/06/28/stanley-mcchrystal-retiri_n_628463.html. (accessed March 15, 2011).

[46] Rest and Recuperation Leave Program, http://www.armyg1.army.mil/randr/faq.asp (accessed March 16, 2001).

[47] Ibid.

[48] Bowker, *The Complete Bible Handbook*, 57.

[49] National Crime Prevention Council, http://www.ncpc.org/cyberbullying (accessed March 19, 2011).

[50] "Suicide of Megan Meier", Wikipedia, http://en.wikipedia.org/wiki/Suicide_of_Megan_Meier (accessed March 15, 2011).

[51] Fred Lucas, (March 10, 2011) Obama Warns About Dangers of Bullying in School and on Internet, CBS News, http://www.cnsnews.com/news/article/obama-warns-about-dangers-bullying-school (accessed March 19, 2011).

[52] Ibid.

[53] Ibid.

[54] E-School News, "Obama pledges crackdown on cyber bullying", http://www.eschoolnews.com/2011/03/15/obama-pledges-crackdown-on-cyberbullying/3/? (accessed March 19, 2011).

[55] Ibid.

[56] Bowker, *The Complete Bible Handbook*, 57.

[57] Office of the Chief of Public Affairs, U.S. Army Training and Doctrine Command, "Army Values", http://www.tradoc.army.mil/PAO/ArmyValues/ArmyValues.htm (accessed March 22, 2011).

[58] Ibid.

[59] Bowker, *The Complete Bible Handbook*, 57.